The Official RANGERS Annual 2008

Written By Douglas Russell

A Grange Publication

ISBN 978-1-905426-92-8

£6.99

Contents

Walter Smith

When the announcement came in January 2007, it was as if the spring sun had arrived early - Rangers legend Walter Smith (architect of 9 in a Row) was returning to his spiritual home.

Born in 1948, Smith was a boyhood Rangers fan and began his football career with Ashfield Juniors before signing for Dundee United as a part-timer (he was also working as an electrician) in 1966. Hindered by a pelvic injury years later at the age of 29, he joined the coaching staff at the Club before eventually becoming assistant manager under Jim McLean. At international level, with the SFA, he was initially in charge of the Under 18 team, then the Under 21 team and assistant to Alex Ferguson at the 1986 Mexico World Cup. By the beginning of the following 1986/87 period, Smith was in the Ibrox dugout as second-in-command to new Rangers boss Graeme Souness and that partnership led the Club to championship glory at the end of their first season together.

Walter Smith first became manager of Rangers in April 1991 when Souness decided to head south and join Liverpool. At that time, the League race was still very much in the balance with Rangers just one point ahead of Aberdeen and four games left to play. This memorable championship was eventually confirmed on the last day of the campaign with a famous 2-0 'walking-wounded' win over Aberdeen at Ibrox. After that, a further seven successive League titles were captured with the last of these – the holy grail of nine-in-a-row – realised at Tannadice in 1997. During this exceptional period, Smith's side also lifted both the Scottish Cup and League Cup

A most-welcome return to Rangers

three times with Season 1992/93 being particularly pleasing for the fans as it featured both a domestic treble in addition to a glorious, unbeaten run in the Champions League tournament. Indeed, during that 1992/93 campaign, Rangers never tasted defeat at all from the middle of August until the following March – a run of 44 unbeaten fixtures that included 29 Scottish League games.

After confirming (in October 1997) that he was stepping down as manager at the end of the 1997/98 campaign, the season ended disappointingly with second place in the Championship and defeat at the hands of Hearts on Scottish Cup Final day. Smith was then in charge of Everton from 1998 until 2002. A subsequent successful spell as Scotland boss (December 2004 – January 2007) ended with his most-welcome return to Ibrox where his first game at the helm was a comprehensive 5-0 home victory over Dundee United.

Walter Smith was back!

> " Smith's side also lifted both the Scottish Cup and League Cup three times... "

2006/07 –
A Season of Two Halves

July/August

Paul Le Guen became only the second Rangers manager in twenty years - the other was Walter Smith - to record a win in his first League outing. Although this 2-1 victory over Motherwell ensured all three SPL points, the final score was hardly a true reflection of the afternoon's events at Fir Park. Leading 1-0 at the break (courtesy of Libor Sionko's eighth minute strike), the Light Blues created several gilt-edged chances during the first half and really should have been out of sight. Captain for the day Dado Prso eventually claimed the winner with a powerful penalty box header after the home side had equalised early in the second period.

At Ibrox, numerous first-half, clear-cut chances were once again squandered but this time the outcome was more costly. Indeed, Dundee United led 1-0 at the interval before doubling their tally early in the second period. Although substitute Chris Burke pulled one back with a super left-foot drive from twenty yards, the game eventually ended 2-2 after a bizarre own-goal by the visitors.

Away to injury-hit Dunfermline, Rangers had the chance to go top of the SPL but the side could only manage a 1-1 draw. Thomas Buffel's second-half opener was cancelled-out after a defensive blunder gifted the Fifers their first point of the League campaign.

With four points now dropped in the first three games, the home clash with leaders Hearts assumed even greater significance but the side (with on-loan Manchester United youngsters Lee Martin and Phil Bardsley in the starting line-up) did not disappoint. Two Kris Boyd second-half goals - a penalty and close range header - eventually separated the teams on a day when there was not a single weakness in blue. The following week at Rugby Park, Kris Boyd hit another brace but a double response – including an injury-time penalty right at the end – meant that the game ended 2-2.

September

Against Falkirk at Ibrox, Phil Bardsley's opener - a stunning Beckham-style free-kick that curled and dipped before finding the bottom corner – was followed by goals from Prso, Boyd and substitute Buffel. Barry Ferguson's return to competitive action (after replacing Sionko at the start of the second period) was another plus on the day and greeted with as much acclaim as any of the quartet of goals. Although Hibernian's 2-1 home victory suggested a close encounter, the Easter Road side completely dominated this capital clash. Filip Sebo (with his first SPL goal) netted for the Light Blues.

Away to Dunfermline in the CIS Cup, Rangers moved up a gear in the second period of the game and scored twice. Although the opener was a wicked deflection off defender Bamba following Hutton's speculative drive in a crowded penalty area, the second – Kris Boyd's stunning 25 yard volley from a long McGregor clearance – was simply the best and an early contender for goal of the season.

More SPL disappointment followed in the east end of Glasgow six days later, however, when Celtic ran out comfortable 2-0 victors in the first Old Firm clash of the campaign. Rangers, without a goal in the last five derby encounters, had now won only four of the previous 22 League meetings between the two great rivals. An additional concern to all friends of the Club was the fact that Rangers had made the worst start to a League season since the early nineties when the 'three points for a win' ruling was first introduced.

October

Aberdeen survived wave after wave of attacks at Ibrox and the game seemed to be heading towards a no score draw before, right at the end, substitute Sebo lit the blue touch paper for a crucial 1-0 victory. Having qualified for the group stage of the UEFA Cup competition less than three days earlier, October and autumn had been welcomed in winning fashion. It was all quite different, however, two weeks later when Inverness CT recorded their first-ever win over Rangers (1-0) on a Govan day when the Light Blues were a poor shadow of the team that had started the League campaign so impressively against Motherwell. Then, three days after claiming the winner in Italy on European duty, Nacho Novo underlined his heroic status by doing exactly the same in the Paisley clash with St Mirren. Charlie Adam (against the side he starred for the previous season) and Thomas Buffel also scored in a closely contested 3-2 win after the visitors had fallen behind early-on. Rangers, failing to impress in successive home games, then lost further ground in the SPL race when Motherwell avoided defeat at Ibrox for the first time since September 1997 after recording a 1-1 draw. Kris Boyd's first-half opener was cancelled-out by Kerr early in the second period.

November

At Tannadice, Rangers - for the fourth time in 13 League games - failed to hold a winning position and were derailed 2-1 after Charlie Adam (four goals in five games) had opened the scoring against Dundee United early in the second-half. Then, at the quarter-final stage of the CIS Cup tournament, St Johnstone's 2-0 win meant that for the first time in their illustrious 134 year history, Rangers lost to a lower League side at Ibrox in a knockout cup competition.

Kris Boyd came off the bench to net in the Ibrox clash with bottom-of-the-League Dunfermline before Stevie Smith blasted home his first senior goal for the Club to make certain of all three points. Novo's long range, second-half strike against Hearts was the only goal of the game at Tynecastle and ensured back-to-back wins for the first time in the current League campaign. Second spot in the table was retained following an efficient 3-0 victory over Kilmarnock at Ibrox. Goals from Adam (a thunderous right foot drive), Boyd (25th League goal in 34 games for Rangers and now second, with 89 strikes, behind Henrik Larsson in the SPL goals table) and Prso (a well-deserved standing ovation when he was substituted late-on) did all the damage.

December

November's mini-revival was brought to an abrupt end at Westfield when ex-Ranger Mark Twaddle netted the only goal of the game for Falkirk. In atrocious, winter-monsoon weather conditions, Le Guen's men struggled to adapt and disappointed in the extreme.

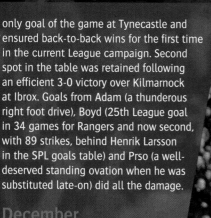

However, against Hibernian six days later, the Ibrox faithful were treated to a quite wonderful 4-4-2 display of pressing, free-flowing football, sweeping aside John Collins' side in an emphatic 3-0 win. First-half goals from Prso, Sionko and man-of-the-match Barry Ferguson (his constant runs beyond the strikers were a joy to see) certainly lifted the spirits in advance of the visit by runaway SPL leaders Celtic for the second Old Firm fixture of the campaign. That Sunday high noon clash of the Titans ended 1-1 after Brahim Hemdani's late twenty-yard strike (his first-ever Rangers goal) cancelled-out Gravesen's first-half opener.

Rangers then headed north to Pittodrie to face second-in-the-table Aberdeen two days before Christmas for another crucial lunchtime encounter. Novo's first-half opener was quickly followed by another from Sionko and the two-goal margin was retained until late-on when Lovell netted for the home side. Hopes of consecutive away wins were dashed at the Caledonian Stadium when Rankin's injury-time strike right at the end of the game confirmed a 2-1 Inverness CT triumph. The year ended with further disappointment after St Mirren drew 1-1 at Ibrox. Despite Kris Boyd scoring after just twenty minutes to cancel-out the visitors' early opener, the winner failed to materialise.

January

A second-half Boyd penalty was the only goal of a hard-fought Fir Park clash and just enough to secure all three points against Motherwell when Allan McGregor, not for the first time, was quite outstanding between the posts. This was Paul Le Guen's last game before he left the Club. With reserve coach Ian Durrant in charge for the Scottish Cup tie at East End Park, Rangers fans watched in disbelief as Dunfermline romped to a 3-0 lead in some 46 minutes of play. A subsequent Kris Boyd double was not enough to ensure survival in the tournament.

... the Ibrox faithful were treated to a quite wonderful 4-4-2 display of pressing, free-flowing football "

Season 2006/07 –
A New Beginning

With Walter Smith now back at the helm, a rejuvenated Rangers romped to a 5-0 win over Dundee United on a day when even torrential rain could not dampen the spirits. Flanked by Ally McCoist (assistant manager) and Kenny McDowall (first-team coach) in the dugout, Smith saw his new charges chalk-up their biggest win of the season. First-half strikes from Adam and Burke were complemented by second forty-five goals from both Boyd (a double) and team captain Barry Ferguson. Central defender David Weir made an impressive debut away to Dunfermline when Adam's early goal - from Novo's inviting ball across the penalty area - was enough to ensure all three points. Although the defence stood firm at Ibrox for the third clean sheet in consecutive matches, Hearts did enough at the other end to earn a share of the spoils at 0-0.

February

Kris Boyd became the first SPL player to hit 20 goals this season when his hat-trick (two superbly struck penalties either side of a well-placed header) buried Kilmarnock 3-1 at Rugby Park. The following Sunday, Boyd struck again against Falkirk on the newly laid Ibrox turf but it was Barry Ferguson who ultimately came to the rescue, hitting the winner shortly after the visitors had drawn level at 1-1 midway through the second period.

March

Midfielder Charlie Adam, taking his season's tally to ten, was the hero of the day with both goals in the crucial 2-0 Easter Road win. In four minutes, his superbly judged free kick caught keeper Simon Brown out of position before, on the hour mark, another set piece strike was this time fumbled by the Hibernian stopper for Rangers' second of the afternoon. In the east end of Glasgow the following Sunday, Rangers certainly rode their luck somewhat in the first forty-five of the clash with Celtic. However, after Ugo Ehiogu scored four minutes after the break with a stunning overhead kick from 12 yards, Walter Smith's side began to play with greater purpose and ended the game far more in control, securing their first Old Firm win in six matches. If the League campaign had started with Walter Smith's first game in charge, Rangers — 19 points out of a possible 21 - would now be top of the SPL!

With Aberdeen only four points behind Rangers in the race for second place and that lucrative Champions League spot, the Ibrox clash was naturally important. Right from the start, however, there was really only one team in it. Kris Boyd once again

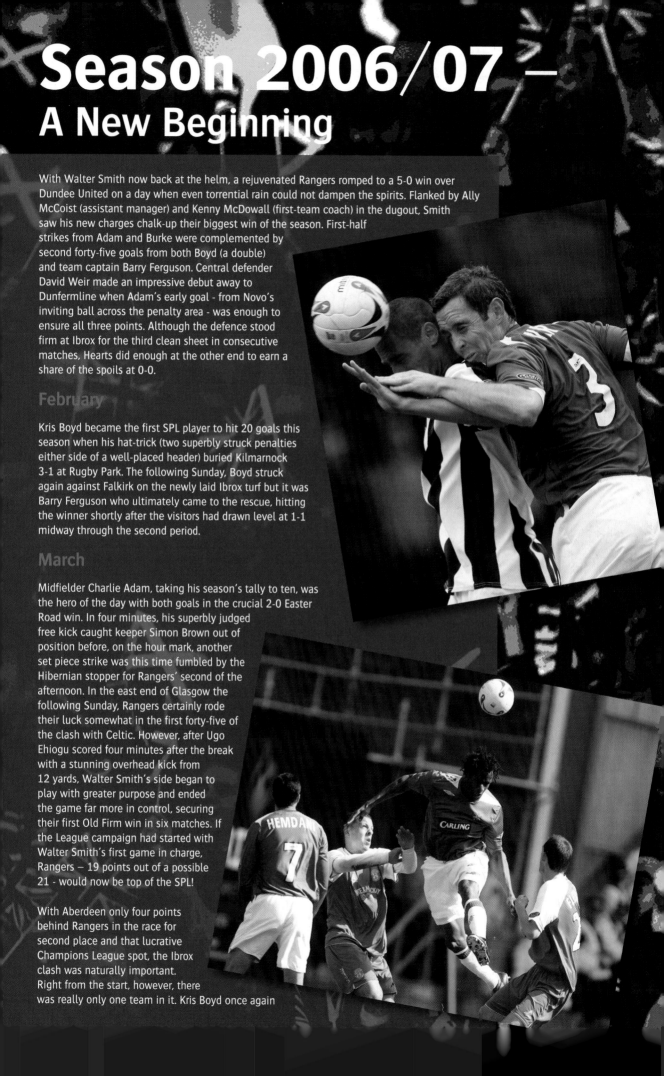

proved to be a master of his craft and, with head, left foot and right foot, hit a sublime first-half hat-trick that destroyed the Dons and silenced a few more of his critics. The build-up play to goal number three involving both Ferguson and Hutton was particularly satisfying. Incidentally, Boyd – still only 23 – was now only one short of the 100 SPL goal mark.

It certainly looked as if Charlie Adam's early goal – a superbly struck free kick – would set Rangers on the road to a convincing victory over Inverness CT. After all, the visitors were already down to ten men at that stage after the dismissal of defender Dods following a last-man challenge on Kris Boyd. The Light Blues failed to capitalise, however, leaving the door open and the team from the north equalised near the end.

April

Away to relegation battlers St Mirren in the final game before the League split, Nacho Novo took advantage of a collision between goalkeeper and central defender and blasted home from close range early-on for the only goal of the game. David Weir was, once again, a tower of strength at the back and deservedly took the man-of-the-match award.

Although the performance against Hearts at Ibrox was not quite vintage Rangers, this hard fought 2-1 win was another step closer to that Champions League spot for Season 2007/08. Second half strikes from Gavin Rae (his first of the season) and Barry Ferguson (a stunning left foot hook shot after controlling with his back to goal) cancelled-out the visitors' 1-0 first forty-five advantage. The magnificent Dado Prso, with another Herculean performance, led the line with all the drive and determination of a true Rangers great. For the second time in two visits to Easter Road, Charlie Adam netted twice with free-kicks but, on this occasion, the game with Hibernian ended all-square at 3-3. Alan Hutton, with a striker's finish, was the other scorer for Rangers on a day when the team fought back well after going behind three times.

May

The last Old Firm clash of the season was more than just a little one-sided as rampant Rangers made it two League wins in a row over their greatest rivals. Although Kris Boyd (his 100th SPL strike and first ever goal against Celtic) and Charlie Adam (another well planned and executed free-kick from the talented youngster) both netted, every player in blue gave no less than 100% to ensure a marvellous win. With that Champions League place now assured, a win over Kilmarnock was understandably less crucial but, nevertheless, Rangers poor display in the 1-0 defeat disappointed everybody on the day when two true legends, Dado Prso and Stefan Klos said farewell to the fans. The final game of the campaign ended in another loss – 2-0 against Aberdeen at Pittodrie – but at least the travelling fans put on a great show with their ticker-tape welcome to the team.

RANGERS ANNUAL
Player of the Year
Barry Ferguson

When Barry Ferguson was stripped of the captaincy and then dropped for the Fir Park clash with Motherwell in early January 2007, it looked, at the time, as if his Rangers career was seriously in doubt. Within days, however, manager Paul Le Guen had resigned and Ferguson was re-appointed Club captain by returning legend Walter Smith. The new manager's first game in charge was against Dundee United at Ibrox and Barry scored that day.

Growing up, there was only ever one team for the young Ferguson and, during his teenage years, he eventually lived the dream and made his first team debut with a man-of-the-match display against Hearts on the last day of the 1996/97 season. With the arrival of Dick Advocaat for the start of the 1998/99 period, his career really began to blossom and he was a part of the Dutchman's side that famously lifted the domestic treble at the end of that memorable campaign. Then, under Alex McLeish in 2001/02, the heart on sleeve midfielder became the Club's youngest ever captain and led the team to a double of League Cup and Scottish Cup.

It was even better the following year when the championship was regained on the very last day of League action and the three major Scottish trophies once again took pride of place in the Ibrox trophy room. Ferguson was also both the Players' and the Scottish Writers' Player of the Year for this 2002/03 period. A move to new pastures and the Premiership ended, after some 16 months, with his return to Rangers in January 2005 and another last day SPL title the following May. Captain again for Season 2005/06, he played through the pain barrier for much of the latter part of that time before having ankle surgery.

Last season, his first game back – the UEFA Cup no score draw with Molde FK – was followed two weeks later with his first 2006/07 goal when Molde FK again provided the opposition. Although Ferguson claimed another in the early December 3-0 Ibrox win over Hibernian, he began to hit the back of the net more regularly after the return of Walter Smith. Subsequent goals in the clashes with Dundee United (5-0), Falkirk (2-1), and Hearts (2-1) - as well as a delectable double against Hapoel Tel Aviv in the 4-0 UEFA Cup win - were laced with numerous man-of-the-match performances. Worth noting also is the fact that the midfielder's strikes in the SPL fixtures with Falkirk and Hearts (a contender for goal of the season) were the winning goals on both occasions. He ended the season just as he had started the campaign - revelling in his role as captain and leader of Glasgow Rangers on the field of play.

> " ...the heart on sleeve midfielder became the Club's youngest ever captain and led the team to a double of League Cup and Scottish Cup. "

Kris Boyd is the centre of attention following his goal against Celtic in the 2-0 Ibrox win, May 2007

PLAYER PROFILES

Allan McGregor

Last season, Allan McGregor was only one of two Rangers players to be honoured as Bank of Scotland Player of the Month. On loan to Dunfermline for all of the previous (2005/06) campaign, his first game last term was the SPL fixture against Kilmarnock at Rugby Park in late August. Then, after eight consecutive starts, the Scot returned to the bench when manager Le Guen decided to restore fellow countryman (and his first choice for the position) Lionel Letizi. However, after returning to the side in early November for the 2-0 win over Maccabi Haifa, the Scot was virtually an ever-present from then until the end of the campaign. Solid and safe, his Rangers Players' Player of the Year award for 2006/07 was just reward.

Alan Hutton

There is no doubt that, after the return of Walter Smith to the Club in January 2007, Rangers fans began to see the very best of Alan Hutton and the right full-back's subsequent Bank of Scotland Player of the Month award for March was more than justified. During that calendar period, his displays in the games away to Celtic (1-0) and at home to Aberdeen (3-0) were particularly impressive. Earlier last season, Hutton's headed goal was enough to defeat Partizan Belgrade in the Ibrox UEFA Cup clash. Then, towards the end of the 2006/07 campaign, his striker's finish for Rangers second in the 3-3 Easter Road draw with Hibernian was a goal of real quality from an in-form player. At home to Celtic in the final Old Firm clash of the season, he was simply – no exaggeration – magnificent.

David Weir

A member of the Scotland Hall of Fame (he won his 50th Scotland cap against Lithuania in 2006), David Weir played for both Falkirk and Hearts prior to eight successful years with Everton in the Premiership. During that time on Merseyside, he was club captain under both Walter Smith and David Moyes, eventually making well over 200 appearances for the Toffees. The 37 year old initially joined Rangers on a six month deal in January 2007 – he was Walter Smith's first signing – but, in late April, this was extended for another year until the end of Season 2007/08. Following his impressive debut in the 1-0 win away to Dunfermline, Weir (who supported Rangers as a boy) never disappointed in subsequent weeks and it came as no real surprise when he picked up his first man-of-the-match award after the Love Street duel with St Mirren in early April.

Ugo Ehiogu

The England international defender signed an 18-month contract at the end of January 2007 and made his Rangers debut, partnering fellow centre-back David Weir, in the 0-0 draw with Hearts at Ibrox. Earlier in his career, Ehiogu won the League Cup twice at Aston Villa (under manager Brian Little) before joining Bryan Robson's Middlesbrough for a then club record fee of £8m in November 2000. Although his time at Middlesbrough was somewhat hampered by injury – he actually damaged a hamstring just five minutes into his Middlesbrough debut – Ehiogu was there to partner Gareth Southgate in the 2004 Carling Cup final win over Bolton. Capped four times for his country, the towering centre-back became virtually an instant hero with the Rangers faithful when his overhead kick decided the game at Celtic Park in March 2007.

Andy Webster

Scotland centre-back Webster – he has represented his country more than 20 times - initially joined Rangers on loan from Wigan Athletic back in January 2007. The previous year, he had headed south to the English premiership after five years and some 150 appearances for Hearts. His subsequent time at Wigan was limited to four starts for the first team. Unfortunately, his Rangers career started badly and the defender unluckily injured knee ligaments in training at Murray Park and missed the remainder of 2006/07 although he was an unused substitute at Pittodrie for the final game of the campaign. Webster eventually made his Rangers debut in the second half of the end-of-season friendly against LA Galaxy in Los Angeles.

Steven Smith

Following his 24 first team appearances in 2005/06 and subsequent Rangers Young Player of the Year award at the end of that campaign, Steven Smith was an impressive player last season from day one (away to Motherwell) until the late autumn UEFA Cup tie with Auxerre in France – a total of 22 consecutive games. During that period of super shows by the Murray Park graduate, the young full-back also netted his first Rangers goal when Dunfermline lost 2-0 at Ibrox. Sadly, a thigh injury and subsequent surgery meant that Smith was out of action from December until the end of the 2006/07 period.

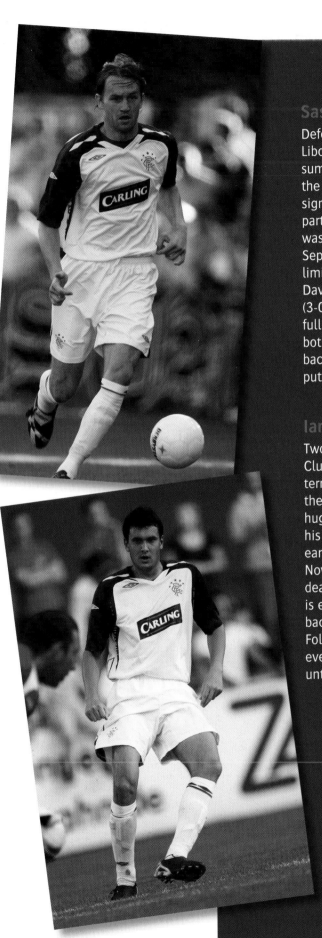

Sasa Papac

Defender Sasa Papac (signed for £450,000) followed Libor Sionko and Filip Sebo to Rangers in the summer of 2006 when manager Paul Le Guen made the Bosnia and Herzegovina international his third signing from Austria Vienna. His first Rangers start, partnering Brahim Hemdani in the centre of defence, was in the CIS Cup win away to Dunfermline in September. Although further appearances were limited, towards the end of last season he partnered David Weir at the back for the games with Aberdeen (3-0) and Inverness CT (1-1) before filling the left full-back position for the subsequent victories over both St Mirren (1-0) and Hearts (2-1). Again at full-back for the May 2007 Old Firm fixture, he barely put a foot wrong in the whole game.

Ian Murray

Two years ago at the end of his first season with the Club, Ian Murray made 37 starts for Rangers. Last term however, after suffering from reactive arthritis, the former Hibernian captain frustratingly missed a huge chunk of the campaign before finally making his 2006/07 debut in the 1-0 win at Motherwell in early January - Paul Le Guen's final match in charge. Now in the last year of his initial three year Rangers deal, Murray, an extremely versatile defender, is equally at home filling the position of centre back, left back, right back or defensive midfielder. Following that return to action at Fir Park, he was an ever-present with fifteen consecutive appearances until the end of March 2007.

Kevin Thomson

Born in Peebles in 1984, Kevin Thomson joined Rangers in January 2007 after Walter Smith agreed to pay Hibernian a fee of some £2m for the gifted midfielder. After establishing himself as an Easter Road regular in the 2003/04 period, the player suffered cruciate ligament damage in a game with Partick Thistle towards the end of that campaign and missed virtually the whole of the next season. However, Thomson was back in impressive form throughout 2005/06 and manager Tony Mowbray subsequently appointed him club captain following Gary Caldwell's move to Celtic. A footballer's footballer, he made his Rangers debut in the 3-1 Rugby Park win over Kilmarnock but it was towards the latter part of the campaign (for example the 2-0 win over Celtic) before the fans began to see the very best of him.

Thomas Buffel

After his outstanding contribution in 2005/06, it was naturally expected that Belgian international Thomas Buffel would again play a key role in the side for the 2006/07 campaign. Indeed, it all began relatively well for him last season and the playmaker netted four times – against Dunfermline (1-1), Falkirk (4-0), Molde FK (2-0) and St Mirren (3-2) - before the end of October. Long term knee problems were a constant companion, however, and he eventually underwent surgery early in 2007, missing the second half of the season. Buffel (capped 29 times by his country) turned down a move to German club Hannover 96 during the January 2007 transfer window and, the following April on the road back to full fitness, re-confirmed his desire to remain at Rangers.

Chris Burke

In May 2006, winger Chris Burke won his first Scotland cap when, as a substitute, he took to the field against Bulgaria in the Kirin Cup and netted twice in an impressive 5-1 victory on Japanese soil. This goal-scoring form continued at the start of last season as the player claimed another, again after coming off the bench, in the second game of the SPL campaign against Dundee United at Ibrox. Disappointingly, after damaging shoulder ligaments during the first Old Firm clash of the campaign at Celtic Park, the wee man was sidelined until the end of the year. Now signed until 2009, Burke's first starting appearance back from injury was the 5-0 win over Dundee United when he scored Rangers second on that January afternoon.

Nacho Novo

The Spaniard's first goal for Rangers last season – indeed his first for the Club in over a year – was the UEFA Cup winner against Livorno in Italy when the Light Blues recorded a famous 3-2 triumph. In due course, Nacho Novo's four goals in the tournament would cement his position as Rangers top scorer in Europe for the 2006/07 period. Three days after returning from Tuscany, with a League game finely balanced at 2-2, the fans' favourite came off the bench to score the SPL winner against St Mirren. Fast forward some six months and it was the same player at the same Love Street location who once again ensured all three points. This time, however, his early goal was all that separated the sides at full-time. Although he did not score against Celtic at Ibrox last May, Novo nevertheless confirmed, once again, that his heart is all Rangers with a tireless display of incredible effort.

Proud to be Captain

It is more than just an honour to be captain of Rangers. Wearing that treasured armband, these six great players became Ibrox legends.

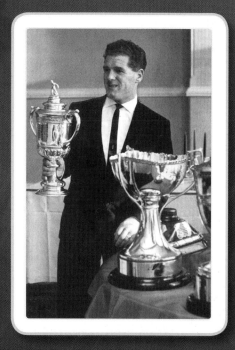

Bobby Shearer

This player's philosophy was quite simple – the Rangers jersey is everything and playing for the Club is the ultimate. Such was the ferocity of his tackling, right-back Bobby Shearer earned the nickname 'Captain Cutlass' and, at one point during his decade at Ibrox from 1955 to 1965, played a quite unbelievable 165 games in succession. Additionally, he became only the second man (after George Young) to captain the side to a domestic treble of League Championship, Scottish Cup and League Cup. Brave as a lion, Shearer whose full-back partnership with Eric Caldow was one of the best in the business, eventually made 407 appearances for Rangers, winning five League Championships, three Scottish Cups and four League Cups along the way.

George Young

This power-house of a man - six feet, two inches in height and a solid fifteen stones in weight - was captain of the great post-war side that dominated Scottish football in the late 1940s and early 1950s. A superb tackler who could also hit uncannily accurate 50/60 yard passes, George Young was a member of the famed Iron Curtain defence at Ibrox. Although more of an obvious centre-half, most of his appearances were in the right-back position due to the presence of the masterly Willie Woodburn in the side. 'Corky'(he always carried a champagne cork for luck) scored twice for Rangers in the Scottish Cup Final of 1949 when a 4-1 win over Clyde secured Scottish football's first-ever domestic treble. In addition to his Ibrox record of six League Championships, four Scottish Cups and two League Cups, the big man wore the dark blue of Scotland 53 times (with 34 of those appearances being consecutive) and was captain of his country a record 48 times.

John Greig

More than any other post-war player, he embodied the true spirit of the Club. John Greig won the first of his five Championship medals in 1963 before being part of the following season's treble-winning team. During the subsequent period of Celtic domination under Jock Stein in the late 1960s and early 1970s, it was, in many ways, John Greig who held the team together and, although injured, he was at Easter Road in April 1975 when the League title was regained after that long barren period in the shadows. Appearing on the park for the last few minutes, the defender was given the true hero's welcome he so richly deserved. Perhaps, however, the abiding image of the man is with the European Cup Winners' Cup on a lap of honour at Ibrox after that glorious Barcelona night in May 1972. After 755 games and five League Championships, six Scottish Cups and four League Cups, Greig's extraordinary playing career eventually came to an end in 1978.

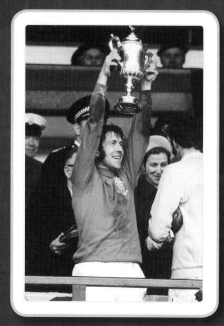

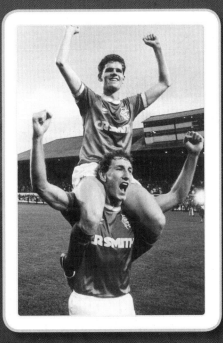

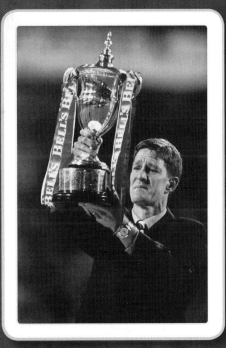

Terry Butcher

One of the most important signings of modern times, England defender Terry Butcher joined the Club back in the late 1980s at the start of the Souness era and, by the end of his first October in Scotland, had led the team to a League Cup triumph over Celtic. The best was yet to come however when, some months later in May, the big man's goal was enough to secure a most valuable point at Pittodrie - and Rangers' first title triumph in nine very long years. The following season, many suggested that the side's championship hopes vanished the November night he broke a leg against Aberdeen at Ibrox in a challenge with Alex McLeish. However, the subsequent campaigns of 1988/89 and 1989/90 ended in celebration and became, in time, numbers one and two of nine-in-a-row. Although he left the Club after falling out with the manager late-on in 1990, a place in Rangers' Hall of Fame was already assured for this true blue Englishman.

Richard Gough

When the nine-in-a-row dream was finally realised at Tannadice on a spring evening in April 1997, there was no one prouder or more emotional than Richard Gough as he held aloft the Championship trophy. Arriving from Tottenham Hotspur in October 1987 for a record £1million fee, the defender was back in the headlines almost immediately when he claimed a famous last-minute equaliser for nine-man Rangers against Celtic in the contentious 2-2 Ibrox draw. By the end of that season, Rangers were champions again with number one of nine. Then, after inheriting the armband from the departing Terry Butcher in autumn 1990, Gough was lifting silverware as Club captain after his extra-time goal confirmed a 2-1 League Cup Final win over Celtic. A total of nine League Championship medals, three Scottish Cup medals and six League Cup medals eventually came his way.

Davie Meiklejohn

The Govan born player arrived at Ibrox in 1919 from Maryhill Juniors and went on to become one of the all-time greats. In time, he would wear the famous colours a total of 635 times, winning an amazing twelve League titles and five Scottish Cups in the process. His status in the eyes of the fans was confirmed in April 1928 at Hampden when Rangers faced holders Celtic in the final of the Scottish Cup, a trophy that had eluded the Ibrox men for an astonishing twenty-five years. When a penalty was awarded to Rangers early in the second-half (with the score still 0-0), the tension in the crowd of over 118,000 could be almost felt. Surprisingly, neither of the regular spot-kick specialists (McPhail or Cunningham) stepped forward - captain Meiklejohn had decided to take full responsibility at this crucial time. His perfectly struck penalty opened the floodgates - Rangers netted another three without reply before the final whistle — and the day was his.

Davie Meiklejohn sits front row, fourth from left

Who Said That Last Season

Quiz

?

Answers on page 62.

> ❝ I look at the dates of birth on the squad list and all these boys are 1985 or 1986– and I'm there as 1974. ❞
>
> August 2006

One

> ❝ Most of all, we have to realise no one player is the most important thing. No player comes before Rangers Football Club. The Club is here forever – all we can do is try to help bring it success while we are lucky enough to be part of it. ❞
>
> December 2006

Three

> ❝ I have just spoken to my mum and dad and said to them that walking out in front of 50,000 fans at Ibrox is something that you dream about as a boy. ❞
>
> February 2007

Four

> ❝ I could not pay them a bigger compliment than to say they have been what Rangers players should be. ❞
>
> May 2007

Two

> ❝ I have no intention of leaving the Club, contrary to what you might read. I have played over 80 games for Rangers and if I get back to peak form I can do a lot more here. ❞
>
> April 2007

Six

> ❝ Seeing him makes me want to play as long as I can. You have to train the way you play and he does that every day of the week. Some guys take it easy through the week but not him. ❞
>
> April 2007

Seven

> ❝ I just wanted to connect right and I thought the keeper had saved it. Being on the floor, upside down, I saw him get a hand to it. It wasn't until I heard the roar that I realised it had crept in. I was one of those surreal moments. ❞
>
> March 2007

Five

> ❝ I ran to Ally because he's really helped me. It's probably the most significant goal in my career. ❞
>
> May 2007

Nine

> ❝ Ian Durrant has been a very influential figure in my life. He made me stronger by constantly encouraging me to keep going, saying that if I continued to work hard I would get my chance. ❞
>
> April 2007

Eight

> ❝ Well done, good finish, that's 26 to go. ❞
>
> May 2007

Ten

Headline News

Rangers made the following football headlines last season. What was the occasion?

1 A Twin Bolt of Blue Lightning
Mail on Sunday, 6.5.07

2 Slov at First Sight
The Sun, 2.10.06

3 What is Sue Gonna do Without Me?
The Sun, 11.1.07

4 Hutt Stuff
Daily Mail, 3.1.07

5 You Only Liv Twice
Daily Record, 20.10.06

6 Hibs' Hurt by a Right Charlie
Daily Mail, 5.3.07

7 Four Four Phew
The Sun, 11.12.06

8 Gers' Early Kris-Mas
Daily Express, 24.11.06

9 A Foolish Own Goal
Mail on Sunday, 18.3.07

Answers on page 62.

Kirk Broadfoot

Throughout Season 2005/06, as St Mirren headed for championship glory, Club captain Kirk Broadfoot was arguably the best central defender in the First Division. Last term, with the competition much fiercer and at a naturally higher level in the harsh world of the SPL, the big stopper never seemed out of his depth and enjoyed another excellent campaign. Born in August 1984, the 6ft 3in Ayrshireman spent five years wearing the black and white colours of the Paisley side and, during that time, also wore the blue of Scotland, having represented his country at both Under-21 and B levels. Many St Mirren fans still recall the time when, back in Season 2004/05 during a heated away match with St Johnstone in Perth, Broadfoot caused more than a little controversy by doing an Andrei Kanchelskis - and stood on the ball during the game!

Alan Gow

An attacking midfielder, Alan Gow was born in Glasgow in 1982 and has always supported Rangers. After three years and over 75 appearances with Lanarkshire outfit Airdrie, he subsequently moved to Falkirk in the summer of 2005 and, almost immediately, became a major player in the team managed by John Hughes. Last season, the month of January was a particularly good period for Gow – in addition to hitting a hat-trick in the 5-1 demolition of Dundee United at Tannadice, he also netted for Alex McLeish's Scotland B team after appearing as a substitute in the 2-2 draw with Finland at Rugby Park at the end of the same month.

Jean-Claude Darcheville

Powerful French striker Jean-Claude Darcheville (nicknamed The Rocket because of his blistering pace) spent five years with Bordeaux at the Chaban-Delmas Stadium and, during that time, became one of the most consistent performers in Ligue One. Wearing the club colours of dark blue, he not only scored 36 goals in 124 games for les Girondins but also cemented his reputation as a real team player. Incidentally, prior to his £5m move to Bordeaux, his strike tally of 19 goals for Lorient in Season 2001/02 included the clincher in the French League Cup Final win over Bastia. Now finally at the Club - both Alex McLeish and Paul Le Guen failed in previous attempts to bring the Guyana-born forward to Scotland - Darcheville has agreed a two-year deal with Rangers.

FOOTBALL INJURIES

1 – Hamstring Strain

At the back of the upper leg, there are three hamstring muscles and the muscle tissue can tear or, in some severe cases, rupture when a player is on the move. This can happen during sprinting on those occasions when the muscles are forcibly stretched beyond their limits. Although warm-up exercises and massage can help prevention, some footballers are bothered with hamstring problems for much of their careers. Any muscle injury requires RICE treatment initially – rest, ice, compression and elevation. Last season, Dado Prso was out for two months after sustaining hamstring damage during the home clash with Dundee United in January.

2 – Cruciate Ligament Damage

Deep within the knee joint at the front of the knee, the anterior cruciate ligament (ACL) connects the thigh bone with the shin bone. ACL damage can be caused several ways, for example by landing on a bent knee then twisting or by direct contact on the knee from an opposition player. This extreme injury requires repair surgery and a subsequent recovery period of many months. Back in 1999, Rangers striker Michael Mols sustained cruciate ligament damage during the Champions League clash with Bayern Munich in Germany.

3 – Sprained Ankle

One of the most common injuries, soft tissue (and sometimes the capsule which surrounds the ankle joint) can be damaged when the ankle is twisted, usually, inwards. Subsequent bleeding within the tissues produces pain and swelling. PRICE treatment is necessary in the first few days following the injury – protection, rest, ice, compression and elevation.

4 – Cartilage Tear

There are two menisci – made from tough fibrocartilage – within each knee joint. Sometimes the menisci can become jammed between the thigh bone and the shin bone when the knee joint bends and the two bones make contact. With enough weight bearing down, a 'cartilage' tear can happen, usually accompanied by swelling and pain. A minor tear should settle with physiotherapy but major tears sometimes require surgery.

5 – Hernia

Hernia and groin problems are particularly common in football as the pelvic region is subject to great stress and force when kicking, sprinting and turning. A hernia (rupture) is usually noticed as a lump in the groin region. It appears when a portion of the tissue which lines the abdominal cavity breaks through a weakened area of the abdominal wall. Although the only way to repair a hernia is with an operation, hernia surgery has improved dramatically in the last decade and can now be performed under local anaesthetic.

Two in Ten
Brahim Hemdani

Ice cool on the park, French-Algerian Brahim Hemdani excelled for Rangers last season - he was particularly effective when deployed as a 'sitting' midfielder in the team - and it came as no real surprise when the Ibrox faithful named him Player of the Year for that period. Maybe rather more unexpected was the fact that he also scored two crucial late goals during that time - with both strikes earning a deserved place in the top ten best selection for the season!

The player started his senior career at Cannes (1997-1998) before moving to Strasbourg for three years. In 2001, he joined Marseille and made over 100 appearances for the south of France club and was captain of the side that made the UEFA Cup final in 2004. Alex McLeish then entered his life and brought Hemdani to Rangers on a four year deal for the start of the 2005/06 campaign. Unfortunately, he was injured pre-season before the beginning of Scottish hostilities and it was October before he made his SPL debut. His first season in the country continued to be hampered by injury problems, however, and he was also missing for some two months during the winter.

With Barry Ferguson out recovering from ankle surgery, Hemdani started last season partnering Jeremy Clement and Charlie Adam in midfield. He then switched between central defence and his favoured midfield role following Ferguson's return to action from September onwards. Regardless of his position in the team however - and despite the side's disappointing domestic form during that time - he rarely had a bad game. Since the change of management at the Club and the return of Walter Smith, the player has been quite outstanding in his holding role, allowing Ferguson more opportunities to push forward during a game.

The first of those two extremely important goals last season came right at the end of the December Old Firm SPL clash at Ibrox when it looked as if Rangers were heading for a 1-0 defeat at the hands of their greatest rivals. Hemdani's injury time strike from the edge of the area initially seemed net bound but a deflection certainly helped it on its way past Boruc in the Celtic goal. Some three months later, under rather different UEFA Cup circumstances but with the score also at 0-1, he was in a similar position to go for goal late-on against Osasuna. This time, however, his strike required no additional assistance from friend or foe and a wonderful curling shot found the back of the Spanish net in explosive fashion.

> "...the Ibrox faithful named him Player of the Year for that period."

Young, Gifted and Blue

Rangers 5 Celtic 0

Towards the end of last season at Hampden, a crowd of just under 11,550 (nearly 3000 more than had viewed the Scottish Cup semi-final replay between Hibernian and Dunfermline at the same venue two days earlier!) witnessed one of the most one-sided finals of recent years at the national stadium. Although there was actually very little between the teams in the under-19 2006/07 League race, this one-off clash was destruction on a grand scale as Rangers swept aside their Old Firm opponents on a warm evening and lifted the trophy for the first time since 2002.

On the road to that final glory, Rangers ruthlessly disposed of Morton (9-0), Stenhousemuir (3-0), St Mirren (2-1) and Ross County (3-0) despite never having benefited from any home advantage from day one of the competition. Celtic's path to Hampden, on the other hand, had been via wins over Cove Rangers, Dumbarton, Inverness CT and Aberdeen.

Billy Kirkwood's youngsters started the game in determined fashion and within five minutes were ahead when Andrew Shinnie hit a super left foot shot into the corner of the net from the edge of the box following a John Fleck pass. Two minutes later, 15-year-old Fleck himself struck the post from close range. Rangers' second, however, was not long in coming and was a thing of real beauty from Steven Lennon. The young striker, with vision beyond his years, spotted Skinner off his line and audaciously chipped the Celtic keeper from all of thirty yards for the goal of the game. Incidentally, Lennon's opener in the semi-final clash with Ross County in Dingwall was also a cracker!

> **...this one-off clash was destruction on a grand scale as Rangers swept aside their Old Firm opponents.**

Ten minutes into the second half, Lennon claimed his second after breaking into the box, having taken advantage of Paul Elmslie's long pass. His hat-trick was completed when he confidently converted from the

penalty spot after Jordan McMillan had been felled in the area. Captain Dean Furman – the ex-Chelsea midfield starlet - then completed the rout some twenty minutes from time when he tapped home after the keeper had blocked from Lennon.

Walter Smith and Ally McCoist, who watched from the stands and congratulated the team at the end behind the scenes, were naturally delighted for the boys of the Murray Park academy. The future may well be orange but on the evidence of this showing, blue can still be the true colour.

Ally –
Super & Simply
the Best

RANGERS Career Statistics

Games: 581

Goals: 355

League Championship
Medals: 8

Scottish Cup Medals: 1

League Cup Medals: 9

Not everybody is accorded a hero's welcome when they first arrive at the Club. Surprising as it may seem, a certain Alistair Murdoch McCoist fell into that category – for he was not always idolised down Govan way. After signing in June 1983 (having previously rejected the Club's advances on two separate occasions), many follow-followers understandably questioned the player's Rangers commitment. However, the striker worked hard to win over the supporters and the rest, as they say, is history.

Ally was top scorer for six consecutive campaigns from 1983/84 to 1988/89, netting 35, 25, 41, 41, 49 and 25 goals respectively. At Pittodrie, on the last day of Season 1991/92, McCoist claimed not only his 200th Scottish League goal but also Rangers' 100th of the campaign when he scored twice and Aberdeen fell 2-0. Also that year, the prestigious European Golden Boot trophy and Scottish Player of the Year awards – from both the football writers and his fellow professionals – occupied positions side by side on his mantelpiece at home. Twelve months later, he became the first player to retain the Golden Boot when he hit 34 goals in the same number of games.

Old friends Celtic suffered at his hands on more occasions than can be recalled but certainly his hat-tricks in the Glasgow Cup Final of 1986 (3-2, 9.5.86) and the League Cup Final of 1984 (3-2, 25.3.84) are worth highlighting as Super became the first Ranger to net three against them in two encounters. There was also, of course, that night of the Glasgow monsoon in March 1992 when ten men in Light Blue defied both the elements and a Celtic onslaught to reach the Scottish Cup Final. Ally was the hero, with the game's only goal.

Two particular strikes feature high on most fans' list of McCoist favourites: the diving header that finally silenced both Elland Road and the English media when Leeds were beaten 2-1 in the Champions League of November 1992 and the audacious overhead kick and subsequent winner, after appearing as a substitute against Hibernian in the League Cup Final of October 1993.

A bad leg break playing for Scotland in Portugal in 1993 put Ally out of the game for some time but, in

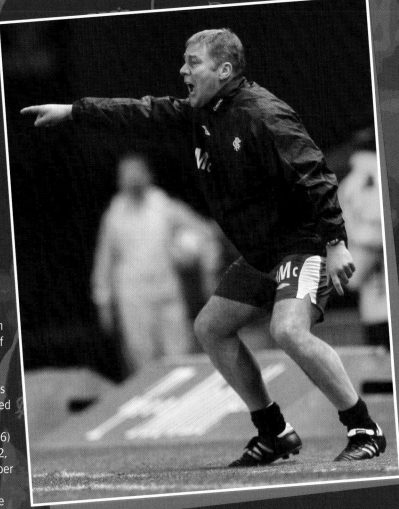

due course, he was back for Club and country and ended Season 1995/96 with 20 goals to his credit. As a player, his time at Ibrox ended with the beginning of the Advocaat period. However, even in his last season with the Club (1997/98) it was McCoist's never-say-die attitude that lifted the team late-on for one final push towards a possible double triumph but it was not to be, despite his valiant efforts.

> **"...he became the first player to retain the Golden Boot when he hit 34 goals in the same number of games."**

Strikers with the predatory instincts of Ally McCoist are a rare breed. Thankfully, at the peak of his powers, he wore the blue of Rangers.

Man of the Century

Kris Boyd

Kris Boyd's Old Firm goal in May 2007 was not only his first against Celtic but also his 100th SPL strike. For the record, here are all his 26 League and cup goals from last season.

August 2006

SPL Hearts (home) – 2 goals – penalty/header
SPL Kilmarnock (away) – 2 goals – shot/shot

September 2006

SPL Falkirk (home) – 1 goal – penalty
CIS Cup Dunfermline (away) – 1 goal – shot

October 2006

UEFA Cup Livorno (away) – 1 goal – penalty
SPL Motherwell (home) – 1 goal – header

November 2006

SPL Dunfermline (home) – 1 goal – shot
UEFA Cup Auxerre (away) – 1 goal – shot
SPL Kilmarnock (home) – 1 goal – shot

December 2006

SPL St Mirren (home) – 1 goal – header

January 2007

SPL Motherwell (away) – 1 goal – penalty
SC. Cup Dunfermline (away) – 2 goals – shot/header
SPL Dundee United (home) – 2 goals – shot/header

February 2007

SPL Kilmarnock (away) – 3 goals – penalty/header/penalty
SPL Falkirk (home) – 1 goal – shot
UEFA Cup Hapoel Tel Aviv (home) – 1 goal – shot

March 2007

SPL Aberdeen (home) – 3 goals – header/shot/shot

May 2007

SPL Celtic (home) – 1 goal – shot

UEFA CUP CAMPAIGN
2006/07

After an uninspired display in the 0-0 draw away to **Molde of Norway** in the first leg, Rangers progressed to the lucrative group stage of the tournament following a nervy 2-0 Ibrox win. Superb first-half goals from Thomas Buffel and Barry Ferguson did the real damage but keeper Allan McGregor also played his part with a man-of-the-match display, denying the visitors on several occasions.

For the group stage of the competition, Rangers travelled to Italy (week 1) and France (week 3) to play **Livorno** and **Auxerre** respectively with both **Maccabi Haifa** (week 2) and **Partizan Belgrade** (week 4) providing the opposition at home.

Italy has been anything but a happy hunting ground for the Club in the past — a total of 10 European ties with nine games lost and one drawn — but history was made on a rain-lashed night in Tuscany when Rangers became the first Scottish team to record a victory on Italian soil in competitive European competition. Goals from Charlie

"...Rangers became the first Scottish team to record a victory on Italian soil in competitive European competition."

Adam (his first for the first eleven), Kris Boyd (a penalty after Nacho Novo had been brought down in the box) and Novo himself (his first in over a year) before the interval set Rangers on the road to a famous win. Although this tie against **Livorno** eventually ended 3-2, the Ibrox men were more in command than the final score actually suggested. It was the Italians first home defeat of the season – even the mighty AC Milan had failed to win here earlier.

Despite some inconsistent domestic form, the Light Blues rose to the occasion in Europe once again and, at the beginning of November, defeated **Maccabi Haifa** of Israel 2-0 following a battling display in Glasgow. Nacho Novo's strike in just five minutes was complemented by Charlie Adam's spot kick conversion right at the end of the game after Kris Boyd had missed an earlier penalty at the start of the second period. Two games, six points and the knockout phase of the 2006/07 competition appeared within touching distance already.

Central defensive frailties were once again to the fore three weeks later in France but Rangers fought back bravely to secure a 2-2 draw after going behind twice on a wet, wet night on the banks of the river Yonne in **Auxerre**. Nacho Novo and Kris Boyd were the second-half goal heroes, preserving the Club's unbeaten UEFA run to date.

This point was enough to take the Club into the last 32 of the competition. However, following the results in the other games, Rangers now actually required just one more point from their final encounter to qualify as group winners. So it came to pass, shortly before Christmas, that Alan Hutton's headed goal in the second forty-five of the match against **Partizan Belgrade** secured all three points and, therefore, top spot in the section.

An injury-hit squad travelled to face **Hapoel Tel Aviv** in Israel where, disappointingly, their unbeaten run of 12 consecutive European games came to an end following a

> "...Rangers now actually required just one more point from their final encounter to qualify as group winners."

2-1 reversal. On the night, Nacho Novo's close finish from Barry Ferguson's off-the-post free-kick offered some consolation.

However, before the biggest crowd of the night in Europe (46,213) one week later, Rangers swept aside Hapoel with a tremendous 4-0 display that secured a place in the last 16 of the tournament. Wearing both his heart and captain's armband on his sleeve, Barry Ferguson scored twice with Kris Boyd (capitalising on some poor defensive play) and substitute Charlie Adam (right at the death after Allan McGregor had been sent-off in rather bizarre circumstances some 15 minutes earlier) claiming the other two goals. The night's opener - an absolute peach – deserves special mention. It involved both Thomson and Burke prior to Novo's cut-back from the bye-line being drilled high into the net by man-of-the-match Ferguson.

In early March, Rangers welcomed last-16 opponents Osasuna of Spain, conquerors of Bordeaux in the last round. The Pamplona side, although struggling domestically in La Liga, entirely dominated the ninety minutes and seemed to be heading home with a well-deserved 1-0 victory before Hemdani equalised right at the end. His 25 yard curler was one of the goals of the season. Interestingly, in the eight UEFA Cup ties this evening, seven of the teams away from home all scored.

Barry Ferguson was suspended for the away return leg and the side, without their inspirational leader and captain, disappointed in the extreme. As was the case in Glasgow, the Spaniards dominated the night's proceedings but this time they won 1-0 and progressed to the quarter-final stage of the competition at the expense of Rangers.

Although out of Europe for another year, the UEFA journey had been for the most part memorable, with a rather wet night in Livorno understandably the highlight of the 2006/07 campaign.

2006/07 Season Quiz

1 Who scored Rangers' first and last SPL goals of the 2006/07 campaign?

2 Rangers became the first Scottish team to record a victory on Italian soil in competitive European action. Name their opponents.

3 Who was the first player to score against Celtic last season?

4 What were the two 'biggest' factors relating to the UEFA Cup clash with Hapoel Tel Aviv at Ibrox?

5 Where and when did Kris Boyd hit his first hat-trick of the League campaign?

6 Name the team that arrived at Ibrox in March looking for their third 2006/07 League win over Rangers.

7 Who hit the winner against Hearts at Ibrox in the first game after the League split?

8 Rangers scored three goals away from home on four occasions last season. Can you name the team's opponents?

9 Three players received red cards in 2006/07. Who were they?

10 How many of Charlie Adam's 14 goals were from set-pieces?

Answers on page 62.

DaMarcus Beasley

Born in Indiana, USA in 1982, speedy winger DaMarcus Beasley was one of the best players in MLS (Major League Soccer) before a $2.5 million transfer to PSV Eindhoven in 2004. As successor to Chelsea-bound Arjen Robben, he was awarded the number 11 jersey by manager Guus Hiddink and, by the end of his first year in the Eredivisie (Honorary Division), PSV had secured their 18th League title with Beasley netting six goals (in 29 games) along the way. Additionally, in the Champions League that season, he claimed 4 goals in 12 games and became the first American to play at the semi-final stage of the competition when PSV faced AC Milan. After two seasons in Holland, Beasley joined Manchester City on loan for the 2006/07 period and, following an initial period of injury in England, scored his first goal – and winner – in the December clash with West Ham. Subsequent goals came in Premiership games against both Fulham and Arsenal. In June 2007, shortly before joining Rangers, Beasley celebrated CONCACAF Gold Cup success as part of the USA side that defeated Mexico 2-1 in the Chicago final of the tournament.

Carlos Cuellar

There is no doubt that when Rangers faced Osasuna of Spain in the last sixteen of the 2006/07 UEFA Cup competition, central defender Carlos Javier Cuellar was one of the true standout performers when he totally commanded his defensive zone with real purpose in both games. Understandably, manager Walter Smith duly took note of those displays by the big Spaniard. The following month in the same tournament at the quarter-final stage, Cuellar's first minute goal against Bayer Leverkusen at the BayArena in Germany was the fastest goal in the UEFA Cup last season. The Pamplona side, in due course, progressed past the Bundesliga outfit to the semi-final stage without conceding a single goal on the back of a 4-0 aggregate victory. Strong and determined in the air with an abundance of technical skill on the ground, the rugged 6ft 3in stopper - born in Madrid, Spain in 1981 – was Walter Smith's sixth new signing prior to the start of the 2007/08 campaign. Cuellar signed a four-year contract following his £2.5m transfer from Osasuna.

Looking back through the Rangers Diary

January

1939 – A record crowd of 118,730 (with another estimated 30,000 plus locked outside!) watched Rangers defeat Celtic 2-1 in the Old Firm derby clash.

1963 – After defeating Celtic 4-0 on New Year's Day, the team never played another game until 9th March due to extremely severe winter conditions..

1987 – The Light Blues had not lost a goal in 12 matches (a Club record) before Hamilton's 1-0 Govan win ended both that sequence and Scottish Cup hopes for the season.

February

1894 – The very first Old Firm Scottish Cup Final ended 3-1 in Rangers' favour. Both teams then headed to the Alexandra Hotel for cup and medal presentations.

1938 – Dundee, although destined to be relegated at the end of this League campaign, inflict a heavy 6-1 defeat.

March

1912 – Rangers secured League title number seven (after winning 1-0 away to Raith Rovers in Kirkcaldy) on the very same day that Scotland played England at Hampden.

1929 – The championship is clinched after a 1-1 draw with Falkirk. At that stage, after 30 games, only three points had been dropped – all in draws at home.

1956 – Floodlights are used for the first time in a Scottish League match as Queen of the South are outshone 8-0 at Ibrox.

April

1947 – Rangers played ten matches, winning nine and drawing one, on the way to lifting the first-ever League Cup.

1978 – John Greig's benefit game was the first testimonial match staged at Ibrox in over 50 years. A crowd of 65,000 paid homage to the legend.

May

1960 – Even a first-leg 6-1 defeat to Eintracht Frankfurt was not enough to deter 70,000 fans filling Ibrox for the second-leg of this European Cup, semi-final clash.

1976 – A week after securing the first-ever Premier League title, Rangers completed the domestic treble by defeating Hearts (3-1) in the Scottish Cup Final.

1992 – Gary Stevens became the first Englishman at Rangers to collect a winners' medal in both the English FA Cup and Scottish Cup competitions.

June

1930 – Rangers ended their North American tour with win number 14 in 14 games, having netted 66 goals along the way.

1962 – A crowd of some 10,000 greeted the squad at Glasgow Airport after they returned from their unbeaten three-game tour of the Soviet Union.

July

1972 – On appeal, UEFA reduced Rangers' two year ban from European competition to one year.

1989 – Manager Graeme Souness announced the controversial signing of former Celtic striker Maurice Johnston.

1995 – The mercurial Paul Gascoigne arrived in Glasgow following his £5.5 million transfer from Italian Club Lazio.

August

1890 – Rangers' first-ever Scottish League goal was actually an og by Adams of Hearts.

1946 – The legendary Willie Thornton (never sent-off, never once booked) claimed the first Rangers post-war hat-trick in the 5-0 away win over Falkirk.

September

1917 – King George V presented medals to First World War heroes at Ibrox Park.

1956 – Rangers' greatest-ever manager Bill Struth passed away at the age of 81.

1977 – Despite being 2-0 down at half-time in the Old Firm derby, Rangers staged one of the great fight backs to win 3-2.

October

1963 – When Morton were beaten 5-0 in the League Cup Final, cousins Jim Forrest (with four) and Alec Willoughby scored all the goals

1988 – For the first time in their history, Rangers retained the League Cup for the third consecutive season after defeating Aberdeen 3-2 at Hampden.

November

1978 – Despite scoring first, PSV Eindhoven were beaten 3-2 in Holland. It was the first time that the Dutch side had lost at home in any European competition.

1989 – Following his first (and winning) goal against former club Celtic, Maurice Johnston's extended celebrations earned him a yellow card.

1992 – Many thousands of Leeds' fans give Rangers a standing ovation at the end of the 2-1 Champions League win at Elland Road.

December

1898 – Rangers' 10-0 thrashing of Hibernian on Christmas Eve was, not surprisingly, both the Ibrox side's biggest League win and Hibernian's biggest-ever League defeat.

1978 – Celtic had appeared in every League Cup Final since 1964 before Rangers ended the sequence by winning (3-2) at the semi-final stage of this year's competition.

Great Goals
of Season 2006/07...

(See the best goal of the season on page 56)

Kris Boyd – away to Dunfermline
September 2006

Not too many of Kris Boyd's goals fall into the 'spectacular' category but this heart-stopping one certainly did. With Rangers leading 1-0 at East End Park well into the second period, Allan McGregor launched a long ball deep into the Dunfermline half that Boyd collected some 25 yards from goal. Spinning, he unleashed a venomous shot that dipped just below the bar to leave keeper De Vries absolutely astonished and slightly shell-shocked.

Kris Boyd – away to Auxerre
November 2006

This goal, after Rangers had twice gone behind in Auxerre, preserved their unbeaten run in the UEFA Cup. With less than ten minutes remaining, Alan Hutton's ball from the right found Charlie Adam who in turn fed Kris Boyd for the striker to decisively drive past Cool in the French goal.

Filip Sebo – home to Aberdeen
October 2006

As supporters checked their watches all round Ibrox, this game seemed to be heading for a disappointing, goalless conclusion despite Rangers' clear dominance on the day. Then, with just two minutes left to play, a Buffel blocked effort fell to Filip Sebo who clinically fired home low into the corner of the net. Needless to say, this - the Slovakian's first Ibrox goal - was greeted with more than just a little joy in the stands!

48

Brahim Hemdani –
home to Celtic
December 2006

Another late, late goal! Although Rangers had commanded this second Old Firm clash of the League campaign the Light Blues, following Gravesen's first half strike, remained 1-0 down with full time rapidly approaching. Then, with no time to spare, Brahim Hemdani pounced on a loose ball on the edge of the Celtic area and shot for goal. With the help of a deflection, the ball whistled past Boruc for a more than deserved equaliser as the stadium rocked.

Barry Ferguson –
home to Hapoel Tel Aviv
February 2007

After losing the first leg of their UEFA Cup tie 2-1 in Israel, Rangers turned the tables at Ibrox with man-of-the-match Barry Ferguson stamping his undoubted class all over the first of that night's four goals. Following good link-up play, he met Nacho Novo's subsequent cut-back from the bye-line perfectly and, without breaking stride, fired the ball high past keeper Elimelch with both precision and power.

Brahim Hemdani –
home to Osasuna
March 2007

On the night of a poor collective performance by Rangers, it seemed as if the Spaniards of Osasuna would return home with a well-deserved 1-0 first-leg UEFA Cup victory. Then, right at the death and out of nothing, Brahim Hemdani (not for the first time that season) conjured-up a sensational goal. Forget poetry in motion because his curling shot from outside the penalty box was perfection in motion!

Great Goals of Season 2006/07 Continued...

(See the best goal of the season on page 56)

Charlie Adam – away to Hibernian
March 2007

Right at the start of this Easter Road fixture, a foul on Kris Boyd resulted in a free-kick some 25 yards out from the Hibernian goal. Charlie Adam, over the ball, noticed keeper Brown in the middle of his goal, probably expecting a cross into the crowded area. The young Ranger, alert as ever, then curled a perfect ball away from Brown and into the net at the near post to the absolute delight of the visiting support.

Ugo Ehiogu – away to Celtic
March 2007

Sometimes the unlikeliest heroes emerge from the shadows. At the beginning of the second period of this Old Firm League game, David Weir twice won headers from a Charlie Adam corner before Ugo Ehiogu, surrounded by defenders in green, twisted and angled his body to deliver a powerful overhead kick that Boruc could only help on its way to the back of the net. Make no mistake, this was finishing that a world class striker would have been proud of!

Kris Boyd – home to Celtic
May 2007

This was one for the record books – Kris Boyd's first ever Old Firm goal and his 100th in the SPL. Cleverly staying onside, his left foot volley – following Nacho Novo's lofted pass – was not the cleanest of hits but it still managed to beat Boruc for the first goal in a well-deserved 2-0 win. For many, his subsequent celebration run to Ally McCoist in the Rangers dugout was worth the price of admission money alone.

Lee McCulloch

When Lee McCulloch joined Wigan from Motherwell in 2001, the English Division Two side (as they were at that time) paid a club record fee of £700,000 for the services of the young Scot. Following the club's subsequent promotion to the Premiership in May 2005, the player netted five goals in 32 League appearances in Season 2005/06, Wigan's maiden season in the top flight. One of those goals was the away winner (and only goal of the game) when Manchester City were beaten at the City of Manchester Stadium in March 2006. During that campaign, manager Paul Jewell paid him the following compliment – "He's a centre-forward playing on the left of midfield. Opposition managers tell me they just don't know how to cope with him." Away from the Premiership, at international level with Scotland, the player won his 8th cap in the famous 1-0 triumph over France at Hampden in October 2006. After arriving in Glasgow to agree a four-year deal, the lifelong Rangers fan said -"I'm here to play for the badge. It is undoubtedly one of the best days of my life. My dad used to take me to Ibrox to watch the great standard of football and now I have the chance to play in front of the best fans in Europe in my opinion."

The Helicopter Has Changed Direction!

By the end of April 2005, most fans were convinced that the SPL Championship was lost for another season. After all, Celtic had just won at Ibrox and, with only four games left, the Parkhead side looked odds-on to retain the League title. However, the following month of May would prove to be more than just a little magical!

Rangers knew, however, that victory would not be enough to take the title – Celtic had to drop points at Fir Park as well. Leading Motherwell 1-0 deep into the second half (courtesy of Sutton's goal), it all seemed to be going to plan for the visitors. Dramatically, right at the end, Scott McDonald equalised and then, almost immediately, hit a sensational winner.

" 'the helicopter has changed direction' boomed out from radios across the land, "

1st May, Aberdeen 1 – Rangers 3

Galvanised by the fact that Hibernian had won at Celtic Park the previous day, Rangers produced one of their best displays of the season. Goals from Barry Ferguson (who opened the scoring with a superbly taken left foot shot on the run) and Dado Prso (the first of his double was a classic back heel into the net) did the damage.

7th May, Rangers 2 – Hearts 1

Man-of-the-match Thomas Buffel not only headed home the first, he also created the second for Marvin Andrews in a game that was never as close as the final score suggested. In truth, Rangers dominated from start to finish.

14th May, Rangers 4 – Motherwell 1

Shota Arveladze, playing his last home game for the Club, and Thomas Buffel both netted twice in a completely one-sided match that featured 13 Rangers shots on target compared to none from the Motherwell opposition. Indeed, the visitor's goal was actually an og by Marvin Andrews!

22nd May, Hibernian 0 – Rangers 1

Nacho Novo, with his first goal since CIS Cup Final day back in late March, was the Easter Road hero and it was his most crucial strike (fifteen minutes into the second period of this capital clash) that eventually separated the sides.

Understandably, by this time, the helicopter carrying the SPL trophy was already on its way to Motherwell. As that now-famous phrase 'the helicopter has changed direction' boomed out from radios across the land, Rangers fans everywhere celebrated like lottery winners on a double-rollover weekend.

Picture **Quiz**

Can you identify the obscured Rangers players?

Answers on page 62

1

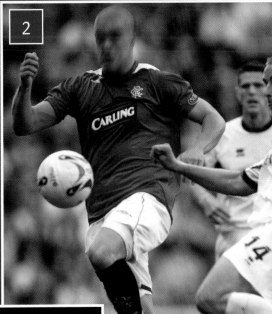

2

3

4

5

A Kind of Magic

Charlie Adam

Against Hibernian in early March 2007, midfielder Charlie Adam was the two-goal Easter Road hero when his two superbly taken free-kicks completely deceived keeper Simon Brown, ensuring that all three points were heading back west with Walter Smith's men. When Rangers, on SPL duty once again, returned to the same ground eight weeks later, it was a different keeper (Andrew McNeil this time) between the posts for John Collins' side. Astonishingly, against all the odds, left-foot maestro Adam repeated the same double dose of set-piece magic and another couple of beautifully judged free-kicks nestled securely in the back of the net to the astonishment of another Hibernian keeper.

The Dundee-born player returned to Rangers last season after having spent the previous year on-loan to St Mirren where he was an integral part of the 2005/06 Division One championship winning side. In Paul Le Guen's team from day one of the SPL race, Adam's first goal of the 2006/07 period (and indeed his first competitive goal for the Club) was the UEFA Cup opener against Livorno on the night when Rangers made history by becoming the first Scottish team ever to record a victory on Italian soil in competitive European competition. Incidentally, that goal in Tuscany was a thumping strike from all of 25 yards.

The next month (November), he netted in consecutive games when Maccabi Haifa (2-0) and Dundee United (1-2) provided the European and domestic opposition. The midfielder also grabbed goals in successive fixtures again the following month as Dundee United (5-0) and Dunfermline (1-0) both fell by the wayside after Walter Smith's return to take charge of the team. By the end of his first season in the first eleven, only striker Kris Boyd had scored more often and Adam's final tally of 14 goals was an extremely impressive return from the midfield position.

It will be quite a time before the fans (and, no doubt, Hibernian goalkeepers Brown and McNeil themselves) forget his four goals in those two fixtures at Easter Road. The opener in the first of those games — the Sunday afternoon clash that ended 2-0 in Rangers' favour - was definitely one of the goals of the season. Make no mistake, his curling ball into the net at the near post had been judged to perfection.

Maybe Artur Boruc was expecting a similar delivery when Adam lined-up to take a free-kick at Ibrox in the May 2007 Old Firm clash. This time, from twenty-five yards out however, the youngster hit a low shot under the jumping defensive wall to the left of the Celtic keeper for Rangers' second of the game.

It was indeed a kind of magic.

> **"...his curling ball into the net at the near post had been judged to perfection."**

Rangers Annual

Goal of the Season

2006/07

Barry Ferguson –
home to Hearts

April 2007

With his back to goal on the edge of the Hearts penalty area, Ferguson controlled Hemdani's cushioned header into the danger zone with his chest and, as the ball was dropping, swivelled and hit a stunning hook shot with his (weaker) left foot that Scotland keeper Gordon could only manage to touch on its way past him. Pure, pure dead brilliant!

Official Young Supporters Club

Rangers Official Young Supporters Club is a super club for young fans aged 16 and under. When you join all members receive a fabulous joining pack containing:

- **Rangers scarf**

- **Water bottle**[1] (4 years old and over only)

- **Manager's note pad, pen & pencil**[1] (4 years old and over only)

- **Broxi plate, bowl, cup & cutlery set**[1] (under 4 years old only)

- **Certificate & membership card**

- **Birthday card & Christmas card**

- **Rangers Soccer Schools money off voucher**

- **24 page newsletter – 3 times a year**

Plus only Official Young Supporters Club members are entitled to some amazing benefits on production of their membership card including:

- **The chance to be a matchday mascot**

- **FREE entry to SPL matches**[2]

- **5% discount on Rangers merchandise in JJB stores**[3]

- **FREE entry to Rangers tours with a full paying adult**[4]

- **We're always working to get our members fantastic discount offers at different outlets – visit rangers.co.uk**

Get on the ball and sign up today!

Membership costs just **£15** for UK and **£20** for overseas residents.
Call 0871 702 1972^, visit www.rangers.co.uk or pop into the Rangers Ticket Centre or any of the JJB Rangers Stores.

[1]Infant pack (under 4 years old only) and youth pack (4 years old and over only). Water bottle and manager's note pad, pen and pencil not included in infant pack. Broxi plate, bowl, cup and cutlery set not included in the youth pack. [2]Offer valid for all home games excluding Domestic Cup ties, subject to availability. Tickets allocated in the Club Deck and Family Section only and excludes Celtic and Hearts games. [3] Discount valid for Rangers products only. Offer excludes sale items. Only on production of valid membership card. [4]Excluding school holidays. One tour per member, bookings must be made in advance via the Rangers hotline only. ^Calls cost 10p per minute from a BT line, other network carriers may vary.

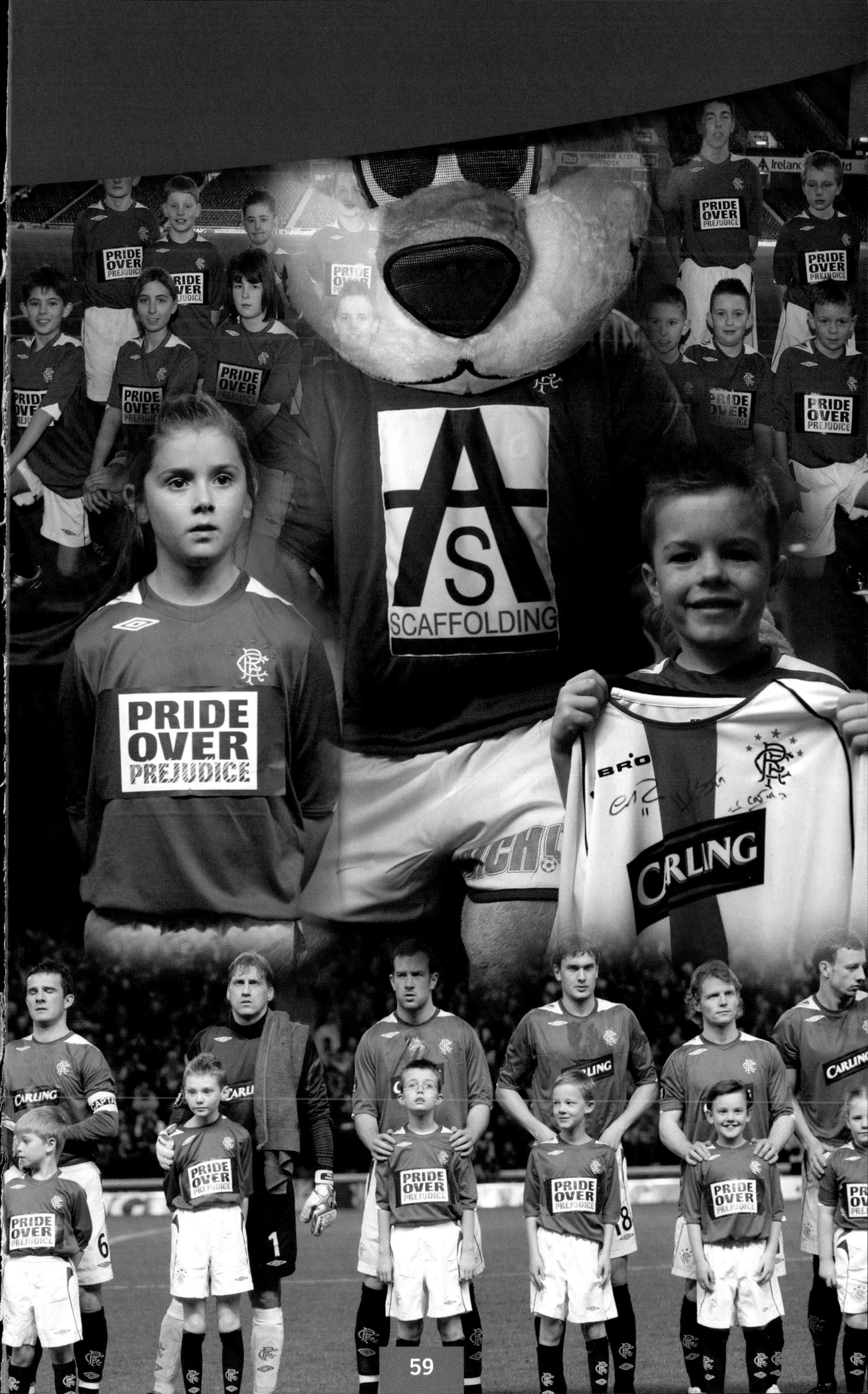
PRIDE OVER PREJUDICE
AS
SCAFFOLDING
CARLING

Nacho Novo celebrates with Ally McCoist after scoring against Chelsea at Ibrox with a blistering drive from 20 yards, July 2007.

Answers Quiz

page 26 -
Who Said That?

1. The great Dado Prso after a predominately young Rangers side defeated Hearts 2-0 in August 2006.

2. Ally McCoist speaking about Dado Prso and Stefan Klos.

3. Nacho Novo after the 1-1 Old Firm draw at Ibrox.

4. Kevin Thomson following his home debut in the UEFA Cup clash with Hapoel Tel Aviv.

5. Ugo Ehiogu speaking about his stunning overhead strike that clinched the Old Firm clash at Parkhead.

6. Thomas Buffel on the road back to fitness following knee surgery.

7. Barry Ferguson speaking about David Weir.

8. Nacho Novo.

9. Kris Boyd after his first Old Firm goal in the 2-0 Ibrox win.

10. Ally McCoist reminding Kris Boyd, after his goal against Celtic, that there is still some way to go before matching his Old Firm goal tally.

page 43
Season 2006/07

1. Libor Sionko and Charlie Adam.

2. Livorno.

3. Brahim Hemdani.

4. As well as attracting the biggest crowd of the night in Europe (over 46,000), it was also Rangers' biggest win (4-0) in Europe last season.

5. At Rugby Park against Kilmarnock in February.

6. Inverness CT.

7. Barry Ferguson.

8. Livorno, St Mirren, Kilmarnock and Hibernian.

9. Dado Prso, Phil Bardsley and Allan McGregor.

10. 11.

page 27 -
Headline News

1. Rangers' impressive 2-0 Old Firm victory at Ibrox.

2. Substitute Filip Sebo claims the late, late winner against Aberdeen at Ibrox.

3. A reference to Question of Sport host Sue Barker after Ally McCoist returned to Rangers as assistant to Walter Smith.

4. Alan Hutton's great display in the 2-0 win over Celtic.

5. After losing at home to Inverness CT, Rangers turn on the style to record a historic European win away to Livorno in Italy.

6. Charlie Adam's two free-kick goals against Hibernian

7. Rangers' 4-4-2 formation blows away Hibernian at Ibrox.

8. Kris Boyd's late equaliser against Auxerre takes Rangers through to the knockout stages of the UEFA Cup.

9. The pre-match comments about Rangers by Aberdeen's Michael Hart are answered with a 3-0 Ibrox win.

Picture Quiz

1 David Weir

2 Filip Sebo

3 Ally McCoist

4 Charlie Adam

5 Brahim Hemdani